WHAT
Was the most brainy dinosaur called?

Om KIDZ
An imprint of Om Books International

Contents

- What is a dinosaur? 3
- What was the world like when dinosaurs ruled the Earth? 3
- What colour were the dinosaurs? 4
- What did dinosaurs eat? 4
- What sounds did dinosaurs make? 5
- What made the scariest dinosaur so scary? 5
- What was the weight of the dinosaurs? 6
- What was the dinosaur with the biggest head called? 6
- What kind of teeth did dinosaurs have? 7
- What was the habitat of dinosaurs? 7
- What were the longest dinosaurs called? 8
- What was the smallest-known dinosaur? 8
- What were the fastest dinosaurs called? 9
- What did dinosaur eggs look like? 9
- What size were the biggest and the smallest dinosaur eggs? 10
- What was the most brainy dinosaur called? 10
- What was the first dinosaur to be named? 11
- What is the longest name given to a dinosaur? 11
- What was the first-ever mounted dinosaur skeleton like? 12
- What was a dinosaur skull like? 12
- What kind of skin did dinosaurs have? 13
- What kind of eyes did dinosaurs have? 13
- What helped dinosaurs protect themselves from danger? 14
- What helped dinosaurs digest their food? 14
- What was the single biggest dinosaur bone ever found? 15
- What happened after dinosaurs became extinct? 15
- Index 16

What is a dinosaur?

Dinosaurs were one of the several kinds of reptiles that lived millions of years ago. Different kinds of dinosaurs lived on Earth at different points of time; some were herbivorous while others were carnivorous animals. Many of them were huge and fierce, while some were small and shy. Dinosaurs are not found today as they became extinct a long time ago.

Pocket fact

Was it a dragon?
It is believed that the first possible dinosaur fossils (some teeth) were discovered 3,500 years ago in China. At that time, people did not know about dinosaurs, so they thought that the teeth belonged to a dragon.

Try this

Which of the following is not a dinosaur? Mosasaurs, Ichthyosaurs, Pterosaurs, Stegosaurus and Dimetrodon.

What was the world like when dinosaurs ruled the Earth?

It was much different from what it is today! Dinosaurs lived around 230 million years ago. At that time, the world was a much hotter place than it is today. Plants such as mosses, ferns and evergreen trees grew at that time. Birds, mammals and humans also didn't exist in that period. However, there were some lizard-like reptiles.

What colour were the dinosaurs?

Their colour remains unknown! Since no real dinosaur skin remains today, we don't know what colour the dinosaurs were. Palaeontologists state that dinosaur skin was probably drab-green shades of gray in colour, allowing them to blend in with their surrounding environments. Since modern-day animals like elephants and rhinoceroses, tend to be dully coloured, many palaeontologists think that dinosaurs had similar skin colour, too.

Try this!

Draw three of your favourite dinosaurs and paint them with colours of your choice.

Pocket fact

We didn't eat fruits!
Herbivorous dinosaurs ate plants called ferns, conifers and cycads. They didn't eat fruits or berries because till then fruit-bearing plants hadn't appeared on the Earth!

What did dinosaurs eat?

Some ate plants while others ate animals! Most of the dinosaurs were herbivores, or animals that ate plants. These include Stegosaurus, Brachiosaurus and other members of the Sauropod family. The carnivorous dinosaurs ate small animals, including other dinosaurs. Very few dinosaurs were omnivores, that is, animals that ate both meat and plants.

What sounds did dinosaurs make?

It remains a mystery! Palaeontologists are not sure of the kind of sounds that dinosaurs made but their skulls reveal that they did make sounds. Some dinosaurs like the Lambeosaur had crests on their head connected to their breathing tracks. The crests were filled with air when the dinosaur breathed. As air passed through these crests, they might have made loud sounds similar to horns.

Find out

How are the coast redwood trees useful?

Pocket fact

I am bigger!
T. Rex was the scariest of all dinosaurs but Giganotosaurus was even bigger than the T. Rex. It was around 15-metres long and 6-metres tall, and had heavy legs that helped it carry its own body weight, which was more than 8 tons.

What made the scariest dinosaur so scary?

It was the Tyrannosaurus Rex, the king of the dinosaurs! T. Rex was a powerful meat-eater. Everything about this dinosaur was ferocious—from its massive 40-feet-long body to its 4-feet-long jaw. It had strong thighs and a long, powerful tail that helped it move quickly. Its massive 5-feet-long skull could pierce into the prey and grip its flesh at the same time.

What was the weight of the dinosaurs?

It varied from one kind to another! Not all dinosaurs were giant and heavy beings. Fossil records show that there was a variation in the size and weight of dinosaurs. The heaviest dinosaur, the Argentinosaurus weighed almost 100 tons. That's equivalent to the size of 15 elephants. Some of the smallest dinosaurs were slightly larger than a chicken, like the Compsognathus.

Pocket fact

Two sets of ribs!

Some dinosaurs like the Tyrannosaurs Rex and Allosaurus had a second set of ribs called gastral ribs on the underside of their body. This set was supposed to keep their body rigid.

Find out

Find pictures of different dinosaur heads. How are they different?

What was the dinosaur with the biggest head called?

It was the Torosaurus! The Torosaurus was known to have one of the biggest head among all dinosaurs. It was a horned dinosaur, related to the Triceratops, which lived in the American West, 65 million years ago. It had an 8-feet-long skull, longer than that of any other land animal. The name Torosaurus means "bull lizard".

What kind of teeth did dinosaurs have?

Different dinosaurs had different kinds of teeth! Plant-eating dinosaurs had long, thin, blunt and rake-shaped teeth. They used their teeth to strip leaves off branches. Some dinosaurs had whole rows of grinding teeth to mash up plants. On the other hand, meat-eating dinosaurs had large, pointed and knife-like teeth that helped them rip meat off their prey and swallow it whole.

Pocket fact

Five layers!

The teeth of different dinosaurs were made-up of different layers. Triceratops's teeth were made of five layers of tissue. In contrast, the teeth of modern plant-eating animals, such as horses have four layers of tissue.

Try this!

Make a model of the habitats of plant-eating and meat-eating dinosaurs. Compare and list the differences.

What was the habitat of dinosaurs?

It varied from riverside to mixed forests! Different dinosaurs lived at different times and in different parts of the world. Dinosaurs in the Triassic period lived at riversides and in scrublands, while the dinosaurs that lived during the Jurassic Period dwelled in Riparian and dense coniferous forests. In the Cretaceous period, swampland, mixed forests, mountains and desert plains were ideal places for dinosaurs to live.

What was the smallest-known dinosaur?

We know them only by their footprints! The smallest dinosaurs are known only by their footprints. It was believed to be a meat-eater from Nova Scotia and was almost 200 million years old. This dinosaur was assumed to be the size of a little robin. However, later on it was believed that the footprints actually belonged to a baby dinosaur. As for full grown dinosaurs, one of the smallest were the little bird-hipped plant-eaters like the Lesothosaurus, which were the size of big chickens.

Pocket fact

Thunder thighs!
Researchers from the Sam Noble Museum discovered the enormously powerful thigh muscles, of a dinosaur in Utah, USA. It was named Brontomerus mcintoshi or "thunder thighs".

Find out

Is the thigh bone the longest bone in a dinosaur's body?

What were the fastest dinosaurs called?

The 'ostrich mimic' Ornithomimids! Ornithomimids were toothless meat-eaters with long limbs like those of ostriches. They were the fastest of all dinosaurs. Some dinosaurs of the group, such as the Dromiceiomimus could probably run at speeds of up to 50-60 kilometres per hour.

What size were the biggest and the smallest dinosaur eggs?

The biggest dinosaur eggs ever found are shaped like giant footballs and are about 19-inches long. They belong to the Segnosaurus, which lived in Asia. The smallest dinosaur eggs are just a few inches across and are shaped like tennis balls; however, it is not known which dinosaur laid these eggs.

Pocket fact

Round or elongated?
The eggs laid by meat-eating dinosaurs were much longer than they were wide, while the eggs of Sauropods, Ornithopods, and other plant-eating dinosaurs were found to be more spherical in shape. Palaeontologists are not sure why it was so!

Try this!

Compare the life cycle of a dinosaur with that of a modern-day reptile.

What did dinosaur eggs look like?

They were of different shapes and sizes! Dinosaurs laid eggs, just like reptiles and birds. Some eggs were as small as cannonballs while some as giant as footballs. Most dinosaurs made nests in the sand and laid eggs in them. Their nests were probably covered with plants to keep the eggs warm. Some dinosaurs also looked after their babies, until they were big enough to take care of themselves.

What were the longest dinosaurs called?

It was called the Argentinosaurus! Argentinosaurus huinculensis was a herbivore that belonged to the titanosaur group of dinosaurs. Its fossils were discovered in Argentina in 1987 by a local rancher. Later, Dr. Rodolfo Coria found more fossils of the dinosaur and estimated it to be 110-feet long and 100 tons. That's as long as 3 school buses and as heavy as 20 bulls and elephants. In 1993, he named the dinosaur Argentinosaurus.

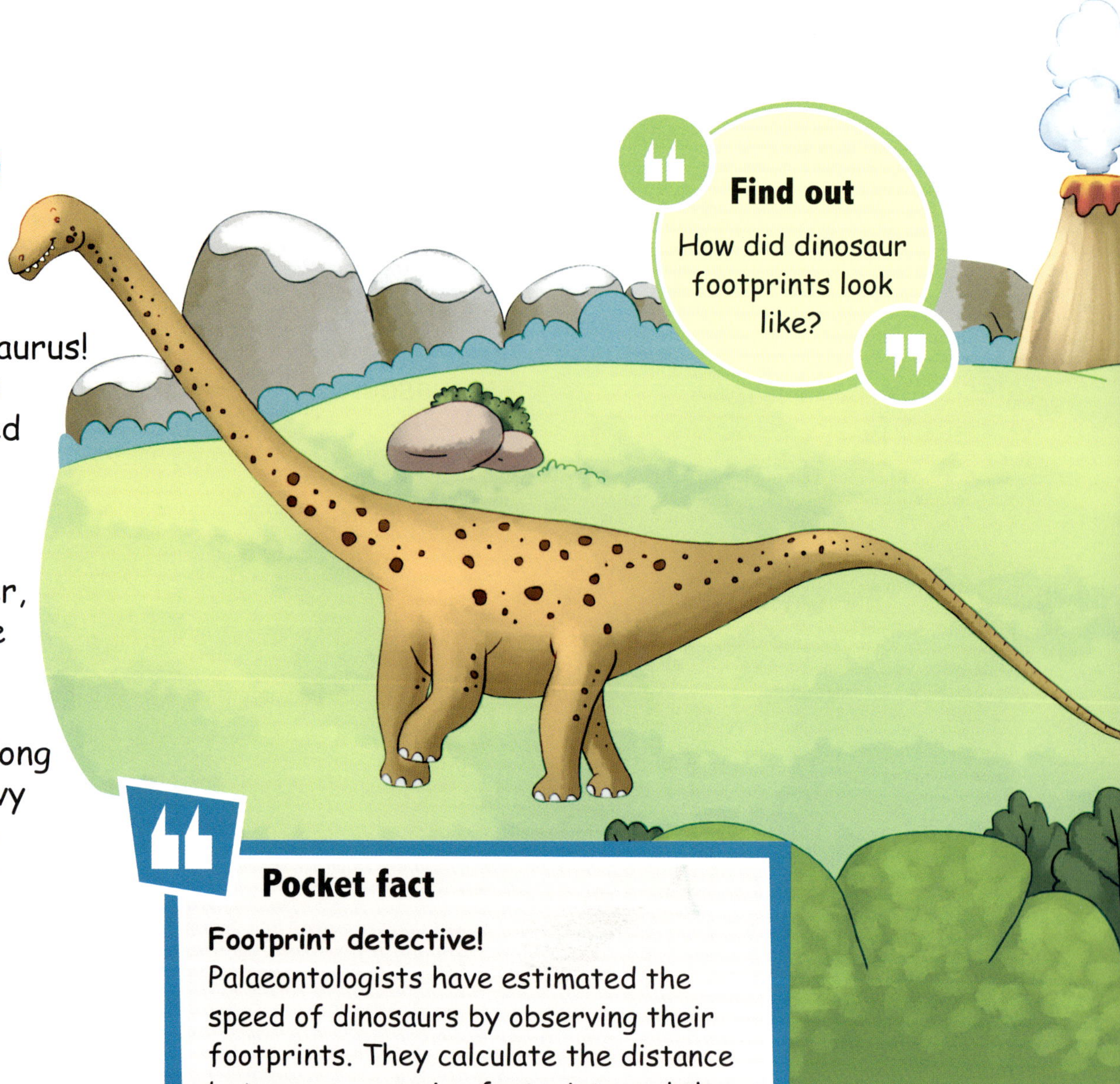

Find out

How did dinosaur footprints look like?

Pocket fact

Footprint detective!
Palaeontologists have estimated the speed of dinosaurs by observing their footprints. They calculate the distance between successive footprints and the distance between prints made by the same foot to estimate the speed.

What was the most brainy dinosaur called?

It was the Troodon! Palaeontologists compare the size of a dinosaur's body to its brain size to get a rough measurement of its intelligence. Based on this, the Troodon has been found to be the smartest of all dinosaurs. It was a meat-eater with a brain as big as an avocado pit. It was not only the smartest dinosaur, but the smartest animal of that existed during that period, including the mammals of the Mesozoic Era.

What was the first dinosaur to be named?

It was the Megalosaurus! William Buckland, a British fossil hunter and clergyman discovered some dinosaur fossils in 1819 and named it Megalosaurus in 1824. It was the first dinosaur to be scientifically described and also the first Theropod dinosaur discovered. Before that dinosaurs had not yet been recognized as a separate taxonomic group—the word dinosaur hadn't even been invented till then!

Pocket fact

What's the name?

Dinosaurs were not only named on the basis of their behaviour but also after the places where their fossils were found or after the person who discovered them. For example, the Aegyptosaurus was named after Egypt where a few of its fossils have been found.

Find out

Imagine that you have found a dinosaur fossil. Would you like to name it after yourself? What would you name it?

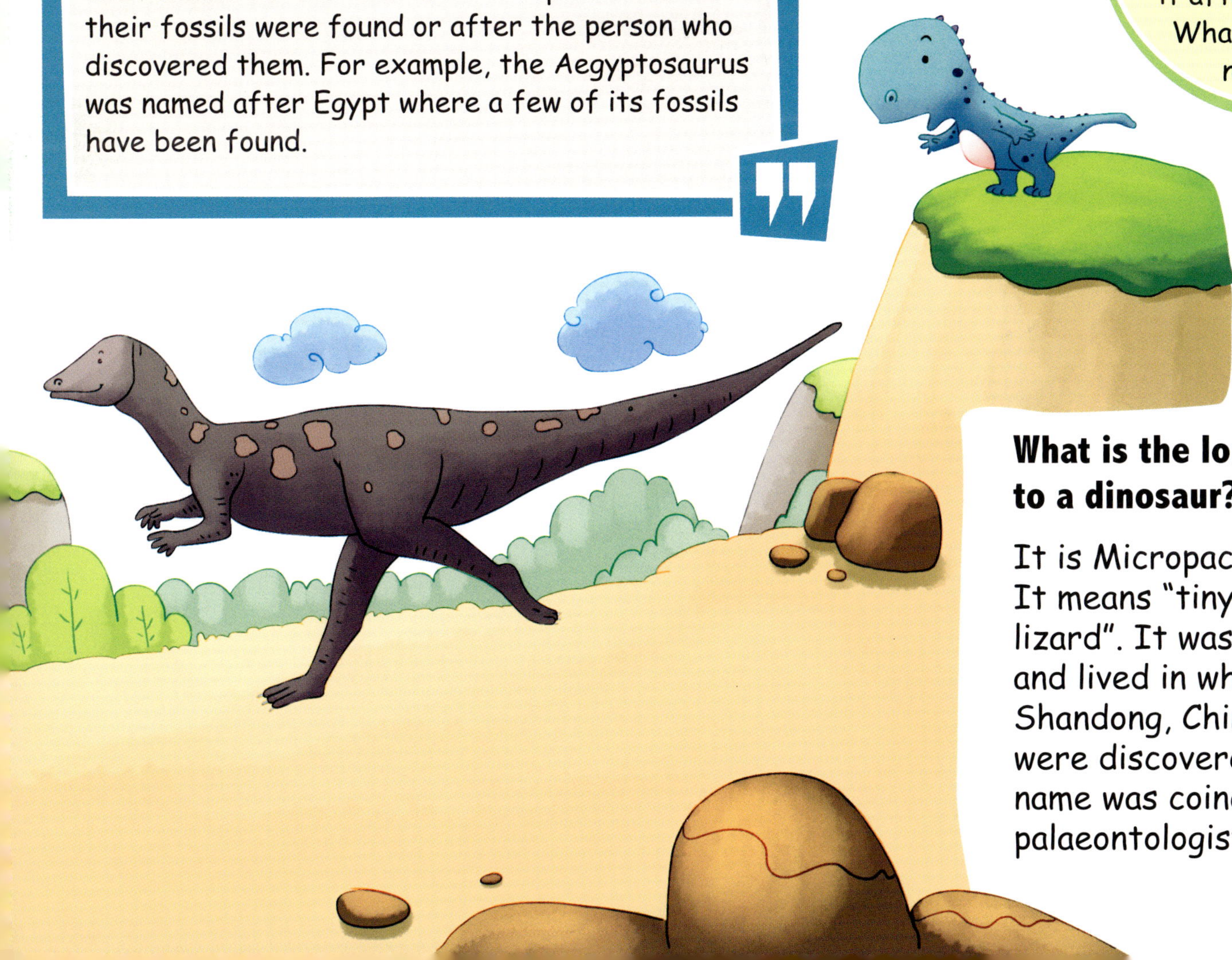

What is the longest name given to a dinosaur?

It is Micropachycephalosaurus! It means "tiny thick-headed lizard". It was a herbivore and lived in what is now Shandong, China. Its fossils were discovered in China. Its name was coined by the Chinese palaeontologist Dong in 1978.

What was the first-ever mounted dinosaur skeleton like?

It was assembled on an iron latticework! In 1868, the bones of a Hadrosaurus were used to create the first-ever mounted dinosaur skeleton. It was put on display at the Academy of Natural Sciences, then located in Philadelphia, PA. Assembled in a life-like pose, the three-storey-high model was the first dinosaur skeleton ever mounted anywhere in the world.

Pocket fact

What a display!
The American Museum of Natural History has more than 136 dinosaur specimens on view, just a tiny fraction of all the dinosaurs that existed in the world!

Find out

What do palaeontologists deduce from dinosaur skulls?

What was a dinosaur skull like?

It had many different features! Dinosaur skulls were divided into parts unlike human skulls that are fused into one large bony structure. Also, dinosaur skulls had two pairs of openings, called fenestra, for the eye on each side of the skull, and two near the top of the skull. The dinosaur skull also had a jaw with five bones and the hinge that is often at the back of the mandible and usually below the teeth.

What kind of skin did dinosaurs have?

It was scaly! Palaeontologists have found skin fossils which suggest that dinosaur skin was tough and scaly, like that of modern-day reptiles. Some like the Hadrosaurs had tough, wrinkled skin with bony plates. On the other hand, Ornithopods had thick, wrinkled skin with embedded bony knobs of various sizes. Small Theropods, like the Sinosauropteryx, may have had feather-like features on their skin for heat regulation.

Pocket fact

Unique eyes!
The meat-eating dinosaur Carnotaurus had unique eyes that faced forward, rather than to the side like most other dinosaurs.

Find out

Did dinosaurs shed their skin like most present-day reptiles?

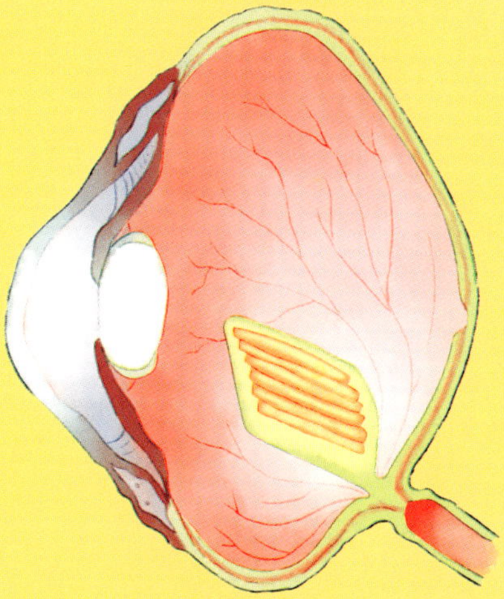

What kind of eyes did dinosaurs have?

Dinosaurs possessed binocular vision. They mostly hunted small and large prey so their vision was restricted to a region largely 20 degrees wide. Some dinosaurs like the Allosaurus did not have very good binocular vision, compared to modern alligators. On the other hand, dinosaurs like Troodon and Deinonychus had better binocular vision.

What helped dinosaurs watch for danger?

Good vision and sense of smell! Nearly all plant-eating dinosaurs had eyes set high on the sides of their heads. This gave them all-round vision which helped them watch-out for any hint of danger. On the other hand, meat-eating dinosaurs had binocular vision that helped them sense danger from long distances. Dinosaurs also had a good sense of smell that was useful for detecting danger.

Find out

Did dinosaurs feed on smaller reptiles and fish?

Pocket fact

Is it an earthquake!

Some dinosaurs were really huge! The Sauroposeidon, a plant-eating dinosaur was named "earthquake god lizard" because it was believed that when this dinosaur walked, the whole Earth shook due to its size.

What helped dinosaurs digest their food?

It was different for herbivores and carnivores! Both plant-eating and meat-eating dinosaurs ruled the Earth millions of years ago. Many herbivorous dinosaurs swallowed stones that helped them grind their food. Also, they probably relied on the bacteria in their gut to break-down leaves sufficiently to release nutrients. Carnivorous dinosaurs had much shorter digestive tracts than herbivores. They relied on strong stomach acids to break-down their meals.

What was the single biggest dinosaur bone ever found?

It was the bone of the Argentinosaurus! The biggest single dinosaur bone ever found was the thigh bone of the Argentinosaurus which was 8-feet long. It was discovered by Diego Pol in the desert of Central Argentina.

Pocket fact

What a price!
A huge T. Rex fossil was found by fossil hunter Sue Hendrickson in 1990. The Chicago Museum purchased this famous Tyrannosaurus Sue fossil for $8 million.

Find out

When did humans appear on Earth?

What happened after dinosaurs became extinct?

The world changed a lot! It is estimated that 75% or more of all species on Earth vanished with the extinction of dinosaurs. Yet many new forms evolved on Earth, which included flowering plants; mammals such as horses, whales, bats; and primates. Birds, fish, lizards also came into being.

Index

A, B, C,
acids
another
assumed
ate
beings
biggest
binocular
blend
bone
breathing
coined
colour
coniferous
covered

D, E, F
danger
desert
detecting
different
digestive
discovered
dully
dwelled
embedded
environments
equivalent
estimated
evergreen
evolved
existed
extinct
eyesight
family
ferns
ferocious
fierce
flesh
flowers
footprints
forests
forms
fused

G, H, I, K
giant
grind
grip
group
habitat
heaviest
herbivorous
horns
invented
knife

L, M, N, P
laid
laterally
latticework
long
longest
mammals
mandible
mash
massive
meat
modern
mounted
mystery
named
nutrients
period
plants
points
position
powerful
prey
primates

R, S
recognized
release
relied
reptiles
scientifically
sense
shades
shaped
similar
skeleton
skin
skulls
small
smartest
smell
sounds
strip
structure
sufficiently
swampland

T, U, V, W
time
tracts
unknown
vanished
variation
vision
weighed